BREAKTHROUGHS IN SCIENCE

ASTRONOMY

BREAKTHROUGHS IN SCIENCE

ASTRONOMY

CAROL J. AMATO

ILLUSTRATIONS BY STEVEN MOROS

SMITHMARK

DEDICATION

■ ■ ■ ■ ■

To the other intelligent life in the universe. May we meet you
someday soon.

A FRIEDMAN GROUP BOOK

This edition published in 1992
by SMITHMARK Publishers Inc.
112 Madison Avenue
New York, New York 10016

ISBN 0-8317-1012-8

BREAKTHROUGHS IN SCIENCE: ASTRONOMY
was prepared and produced by
Michael Friedman Publishing Group, Inc.
15 West 26th Street
New York, New York 10010

Editor: Dana Rosen
Art Director: Jeff Batzli
Designer: Lynne Yeamans
Layout Artist: Philip Travisano
Photography Researcher: Daniella Jo Nilva
Illustrator: Steven Moros

Typeset by Bookworks Plus
Color separations by Rainbow Graphic Arts Co.
Printed and bound in Hong Kong by Leefung-Asco Printers Ltd.

TABLE OF CONTENTS

Introduction

■　■　■　■　■

Have you ever looked upward on a clear, moonless night, scanned the endless stars spreading across the sky, and wondered if there are other planets just like earth out there? Does other intelligent life exist in the universe? Where does the universe end? In times past, people asked even more basic questions than these. What is the moon? What are the stars? Is earth the center of the universe? Is there a crystal bowl over the top of the universe, holding the stars a few thousand feet above earth?

Over the last five thousand years, many people have struggled to explain the mysteries of the vast expanse that surrounds our blue planet. The study of the universe is called astronomy, and it is the oldest science in the world.

Ancient people, lacking any kind of scientific instruments, could only guess at what the heavenly bodies were. For instance, many cultures thought of the moon as a goddess. The Greeks called her Artemis, and the Romans called her Diana, lover of the woods. Later cultures thought of the moon as a mirror and the dark areas on the surface as a reflection of the earth. Many people speak of the so-called "man in the moon," and, not so long ago, many claimed the moon was made of green cheese.

Both the Greeks and Romans believed the earth was the center of the universe. Since antiquity, however, we have learned that we are *not* the center of the universe, nor even of the solar system. Rather, we are a little planet circling a very ordinary star at the *outer edge* of our galaxy.

The process of learning about the universe took many centuries and was frequently met with great resistance from those who could not let go of traditional, often superstitious, views. Unlike some sciences, astronomy undergoes constant change. We are making new discoveries about the universe all of the time, and we must adjust our beliefs accordingly. A little trip back through time will show the many scientific breakthroughs made in the field of astronomy and demonstrate how these discoveries have changed our lives.

Courtesy Nasa

This photograph shows the trail of a satellite across our galaxy, the Milky Way. Our solar system, which includes the sun, the earth, and the other eight planets, is located on the outer edge of the Milky Way. Beyond the Milky Way, there may be millions or billions of other galaxies.

1

THE EARLY ASTRONOMERS

The ancient Egyptians believed that the earth was shaped like a rectangular box, with a pillar at each corner. They thought that under the box was the river Ur-nes, where the gods sailed in boats.

THE MIDDLE EAST

In the Middle East some 6,000 years ago, several agricultural societies, such as the Assyrians, Babylonians, and Egyptians, lived in fertile valleys with rivers that flooded during certain times of the year. To prevent those flood seasons from taking them by surprise and destroying their crops, they developed calendars and began watching the motions of the sun and moon. These ancient cultures organized their gods around their studies of the sky and created them to help make sense of how the world came to be. These beliefs developed into what we call astrology—the nonscientific study of the stars.

The Chaldeans of Babylonia were the first to develop astrology, probably around 3000 B.C. They believed that the power controlling a person's destiny lived in the heavens and that he or she might be able to learn what that power was planning by predicting the motions of the sun, moon, and planets. They thought that each star and planet was an individual god who had an effect on men and women. According to Babylonian astrology, the person's personality and his or her fate in life depended on the sign under which he or she was born and the positions of the planets on certain days throughout life.

The Egyptians made important contributions to astronomy, but they thought the earth was shaped like a rectangular box. They pictured this box having a flat ceiling, supported by a pillar at each of the four corners. The pillars were connected by a mountain range. Below the mountains was a river called Ur-nes. The Egyptians believed that the sun and the moon and the other gods sailed in boats along this river. Egypt was in the center of a flat earth and was surrounded by a huge ocean.

The Egyptians found constellations, or patterns of stars, in the night sky, but they were different from those we now use. The Egyptian pyramids, which were astronomi-

■ ■ ■ ■ ■ ■ ■ ■ ■ ■ ■ ■ ■

Many theories exist about how the Egyptians built the pyramids. Some scientists believe that the Egyptians used thousands of slaves to roll the stones on logs to get them to their locations. We're not sure if this is true. The proportions of the pyramids show that the Egyptians had advanced mathematical knowledge.

cal observatories, were their most important contribution to astronomy. The Great Pyramid of King Cheops lines up with what was the north star at the time.

Other cultures that shared similar ideas were the Indians, Chinese, Greeks, Mayans, and ancient Britons.

THE ANCIENT INDIANS

Like the Egyptians and most cultures through the time of Columbus, the ancient Indians thought the world was flat. Their Vedic priests thought the earth was supported by twelve big pillars, however, not just four. At night, the sun passed underneath the pillars. The Hindus, on the other hand, thought the earth stood on the backs of four elephants. The elephants stood on a tortoise, which stood on a snake that floated in the middle of an endless ocean.

THE ANCIENT CHINESE

The Chinese wrote about planets around 2500 B.C. They also developed a 365-day calendar. They did not know whether the sun revolved around the earth or the earth around the sun, but this was not an issue of importance to them. They thought the world had been created for the emperor of China.

For 2,000 years, between 500 B.C. and A.D. 1500, China was far ahead of the West in science and technology. The Chinese were also very interested in astrology. Their court astronomers looked to the stars to predict future occurrences, such as wars, plagues, and death, so that they could warn the emperor ahead of time.

The Chinese watched for any new stars in the night sky. They called these "guest stars" and recorded more than fifty of them.

The ancient Hindus believed the earth stood on the backs of four very strong elephants. The elephants balanced themselves and their enormous load on the back of a tortoise. The tortoise, in turn, stood on a snake, which floated in the middle of an endless ocean.

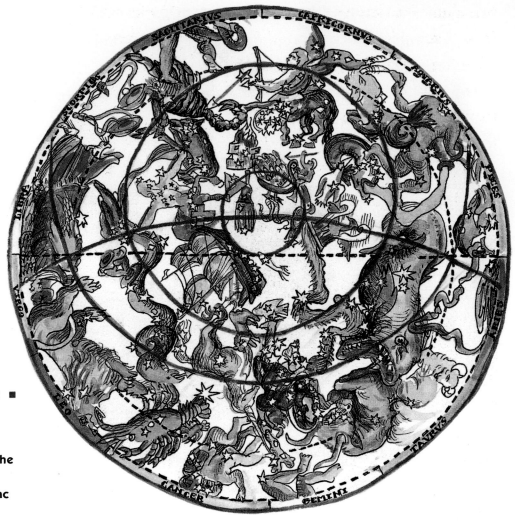

■ ■ ■ ■ ■ ■ ■ ■ ■ ■ ■ ■ ■ ■

The Greek zodiac consisted of twelve regions, each containing a constellation. The Greeks named the constellations after animals and mythological characters. The zodiac is still used today in astrological horoscopes.

THE GREEKS

■ ■

The Greek era is considered the Age of Classical Astronomy. The Greeks borrowed astrology from the Babylonians and Egyptians in the fourth century B.C. but combined it with their religion, which had humanlike gods, and with their rapidly developing science called astronomy.

The Greeks thought that the earth was the center of the universe and everything in the sky revolved around it. The Greeks noticed that five of the stars they saw were brighter than the others and seemed to move. Later, the Romans, who learned much about astronomy from the Greeks, named these stars Mercury, Venus, Mars, Jupiter, and Saturn, names which we still use today. The Greeks called these five stars, plus the moon and the sun, *planetes*, meaning "wanderers."

The Greeks believed the planets were more important than the stars. As true believers in astrology, they, too, thought that the motion of the planets affected humans and the earth and believed if they could predict the planets' motions accurately, they might learn how people would be affected. They divided the path the sun, moon, and planets traveled along into twelve regions, with the sun staying in each region for one month. Each region had a group of stars in it called a constellation. The Greeks assigned animals and mythological characters to the constellations, and together, the twelve constellations were called the *zodiac*, from the Greek word for "circle of animals." We still use the Greek zodiac today.

Several Greek scientists are remembered for their views on astronomy.

■ Plato

Plato (428–347 B.C.), a Greek philosopher, believed that the universe was permanent, fixed, and perfect. He felt that only circular motions were perfect. Therefore, in order to be perfect and still move, the planets had to be making a series of circular movements.

■ Aristotle

Aristotle (384–322 B.C.), a Greek philosopher and student of Plato, felt that while life on earth was born, changed, and then died, the stars were fixed in the sky and never changed. He believed the earth was made of four elements: earth, water, air, and fire, while the sky and its six thousand stars were made of *aither*, or *aether*, which means "blazing."

■ ■ ■ ■ ■ ■ ■ ■ ■ ■ ■ ■ ■ ■ ■

During a lunar eclipse, the earth comes between the sun and the moon, and a shadow of the earth is cast onto the moon. The Greek philosopher Aristotle postulated that because this shadow is curved, the earth must be round.

Aristotle theorized that clouds and rain were part of the air and that the air went all the way up to the moon. The sky and the aether started with the moon and included everything beyond it. He thought shooting stars were in the air, too, and called them *meteors*, from a Greek word meaning "things in the air."

Aristotle made a major contribution to astronomy: He believed the idea of a flat earth to be wrong. He deduced that the earth was sphere-shaped and had three pieces of evidence to support this conclusion. First, he felt that heavenly bodies were sphere-shaped when all parts tended toward the center. This was the first glimmer of the idea of gravity. Second, he pointed out that the stars appear to change in height above or below the horizon according to where the person viewing them stands on the earth. For instance, the brilliant southern star Canopus could be seen from Alexandria, but not from Athens. Things could only be this way if the earth was a globe. Third, he pointed to eclipses of the moon. A lunar eclipse occurs when the earth comes between the sun and the moon. When this happens, the shadow of the earth is visible on the moon. Aristotle claimed that just as earth's shadow on the moon was curved, so, too, must the surface of the earth be curved.

■ Eratosthenes

Eratosthenes (Air-uh-*toss*-the-neez) of Cyrene (276–194 B.C.) takes credit for the first major breakthrough in astronomy—he measured the size of the earth. Using the stadion—an old Greek measurement—Eratosthenes concluded that the earth's circumference was about 28,000 miles (45,000 kilometers). The real measurement is 24,902.4 miles (39,844 kilometers). This is considered the first great breakthrough, because it was not achieved by guesswork, but by careful scientific reasoning.

■ ■ ■ ■ ■ ■ ■ ■ ■ ■ ■ ■ ■ ■

Sometimes the moon comes between the sun and the earth. This is called a solar eclipse. The moon almost blocks the sun, but leaves a little ring around the edge, called the "diamond ring" effect. Because the moon is only 239,000 miles (380,800 kilometers) from earth, while the sun is 93,000,000 miles (148,800,000 kilometers) away, the moon seems to cover the sun, even though, of course, the moon is very small compared to the sun.

■ Aristarchus

The Greeks actually discovered the fact that the earth is not the center of the universe. Aristarchus of Samos (217–145 B.C.) believed this fact, and he gave the sun's distance as 5 million miles (8 million kilometers). Although his measurement was wrong, his theory was correct. No one listened to Aristarchus, however, and his discovery was almost completely disregarded until the Middle Ages, when Copernicus once again proposed it.

Courtesy Nasa

The crew of NASA's rocket *Apollo 17* took this beautiful picture of the earth. This picture includes the Mediterranean Sea area to Antarctica. If you look closely, you can see the coastline of Africa.

■ Hipparchus

The greatest Greek astronomer of all was Hipparchus of Nicaea (146–127 B.C.). Even though he had no tools, he thought of a better system of circle combinations than anyone had been able to do before him. His new system was followed for 1,700 years.

Hipparchus prepared a star catalog in 134 B.C. This catalog described 850 of the brightest stars. He catalogued them according to their brightness, which is called a star's "magnitude."

■ Ptolemy

Another Greek astronomer was Claudius Ptolemaeus (A.D. 100–170), whom we usually call Ptolemy. He summarized Hipparchus' system into a book of his own, along with the star catalog, and added some improvements. As a result, the earth-centered universe system is called the "Ptolemaic" system. He wrote a book called *Syniaxis*, which we know as *Almgest*, an encyclopedia of ancient science, and thus received his nickname "The Prince of Astronomers." He also made the first map of the world. Ptolemy was the last of the Greek astronomers, and with him, the classical era, the world of the ancient Greeks and Romans, was coming to an end.

■ ■ ■ ■ ■ ■ ■ ■ ■ ■ ■ ■

Ptolemy, a Greek astronomer, made the first map of the world. He is known as the "Prince of Astronomers."

■ ■ ■ ■ ■ ■ ■ ■ ■ ■ ■ ■

Through this modern telescope, the craters on the moon are clearly visible. Almost 2,000 years ago, Ptolemy put forth the idea that the moon has craters.

Other Greek scientists also made contributions. Greek philosopher Anaximander was credited with believing that the earth was suspended freely in space. Pythagoras, a Greek mathematician and religious reformer remembered for his geometrical theorem, knew the earth was a globe. Anaxagoras of Claxomenace was a flat-earth supporter but felt the sun was a red hot body larger than Greece. Religious leaders banned him from Athens. He made two major advances: He thought the moon had mountains and ravines, and he understood the causes of eclipses.

THE ROMANS

The Romans had little interest in science and did not share the Greek love of learning. They did take time, however, to reform the calendar. They realized the true year is 365 ¼ days, not just 365. Julius Caesar instructed a Greek astronomer, Sosigenes (Soh-*sih*-jeh-neez), to create a more accurate calendar. Sosigenes invented the leap year to keep the calendar accurate. The Julian calendar is the one we use today.

THE BUILDERS OF STONEHENGE

For many years, people wondered about the purpose of the ancient circle of tall stones that sits on the Salisbury Plain in Wiltshire, England. In 1964, American astronomer Gerald S. Hawkins (1928–) took measurements at Stonehenge and put them into a computer programmed with astronomical information regarding the positions of the stars in 1500 B.C., around the time when Stonehenge was in use. In this way, he discovered that Stonehenge was an ancient astronomical observatory.

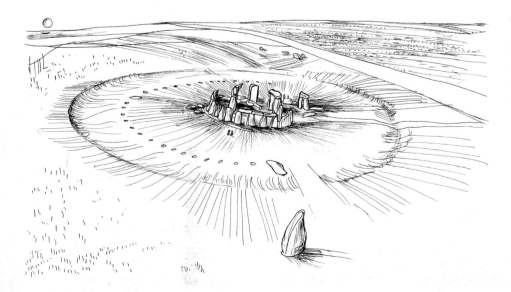

Stonehenge is believed to be an astronomical observatory used around 1500 B.C. by the ancient inhabitants of Britain.

© Bill Everitt/Tom Stack & Associates

■ ■ ■ ■ ■ ■ ■ ■ ■ ■ ■ ■ ■

This photograph shows the massive size of the monoliths at Stonehenge.

Two of the stones at Stonehenge particularly interested Hawkins. On June 21, the summer solstice, or the first day of summer, the sun lines up between these two stones. The same is true of stone arches found in other parts of the world, such as the southwestern United States. (In North America, there are also Native American artifacts called "medicine wheels." These are astronomical devices and have nothing to do with medicine. One such device, at Moose Mountain in South Saskatchewan, Canada, is over 2,000 years old.) The field that studies ancient observatories is called "archaeoastronomy."

Hawkins believes that Stonehenge was an ancient astronomical observatory used to predict the summer and winter solstices, the vernal and autumnal equinoxes (the two times each year when the sun crosses the equator), eclipses, and other information about the sun and moon. Stonehenge can be described as a primitive digital computer that supplied a daily calendar.

The Stonehenge that exists now is really Stonehenge III. The first Stonehenge was built about 2100 B.C. by an ancient British culture known as the Beaker people. The Romans destroyed it between 55 B.C. and A.D. 410. The main structure dates from the late Stone Age or Early Bronze Age and has been rebuilt over the years.

THE ANCIENT MAYAS

When we think of ancient civilizations, we normally think of the Greeks and Romans and the advanced cultures of the Middle East. You might be surprised to learn that the ancient Mayas of southern Mexico were just as advanced.

The Mayas were obsessed with time, because, like the cultures of the Middle East, they were an agricultural people dependent on knowing the precise starting times of the seasons. They used a type of agriculture called "slash and burn." They had to cut the vegetation in the dry season, and in turn they had to have an accurate calendar to know when rainy seasons would come.

Time controlled every element of the Mayas' lives, and they used their calendar to maintain a stable existence. They discovered a correlation between the motion of the planets and seasonal changes. Like many other cultures, they, too, believed that the stars influenced peoples' destinies, so they assigned the tasks of charting and interpreting astronomical movements to their priests.

The Mayas knew the earth had a 365-day cycle, but they followed a 260-day calendar that was actually more correct than the one we use today. It was correct to the fifth decimal point. Ours is correct only to the fourth decimal point. The Mayan calendar reached 374,440 years into the future without a single error.

■ ■ ■ ■ ■ ■ ■ ■ ■ ■ ■ ■ ■ ■ ■

The ancient Mayas were as advanced as the ancient Greeks in their knowledge of mathematics and astronomy. This Mayan monument is aligned to correspond with different movements of the sun. In fact, the main façade faces the location of the last ray of sunlight during the summer solstice.

2

·····

BREAKTHROUGHS DURING THE MIDDLE AGES

·····

Astronomer Nicolaus Copernicus proposed the idea that the sun, not the earth, was the center of the universe.

THE DISCOVERY OF THE SUN-CENTERED SOLAR SYSTEM

As discussed in the last chapter, Aristotle and Plato taught that the earth was the center of the universe, a theory that was not contradicted until the 1500s.

The person who put forth this idea was a Polish astronomer named Mikolaj Kopernik, whom we call Nicolaus Copernicus (1473–1543). Educated at Krakow University, Copernicus was interested in astronomy and concerned with the design of the solar system. He felt that Ptolemy's

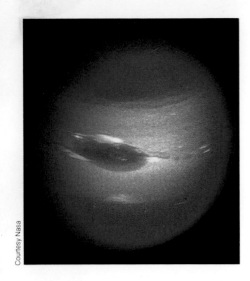

Courtesy Nasa

■ ■ ■ ■ ■ ■ ■ ■ ■ ■ ■ ■ ■ ■

The camera on the *Voyager 2* satellite took this picture of Neptune, the eighth planet from the sun. The picture was taken through a colored filter in order to show clearly details of the cloud structure. The pink clouds are probably at a higher altitude than the blue ones. Neptune, which is seventeen times larger than the earth, takes 165 earth-years to complete one orbit around the sun.

theory of the earth-centered solar system was wrong because it was unnecessarily complicated. Copernicus had more accurate measurements of the planets' motions, though he still thought their orbits were perfectly circular. Finally, he realized that there was only one explanation: The *sun* was the center of the solar system.

Ptolemy's ideas, however, were taught in all the universities. Copernicus knew the professors would not agree with his new discovery. He knew the Catholic Church would also oppose him. Copernicus' theory was complete in 1533, but he did not publish it. Several people, including some church members, found out about his discovery, however, and encouraged him to write a book. *De revolutionibus* (On the revolutions) was not published until 1543. Copernicus saw it a few hours before he died.

The great scientist's fears proved true—the Church reacted hostilely and many people suffered for believing him. In February 1600, Giordano Bruno, an Italian philosopher, was burned at the stake in Rome for heresy, after spending seven years in prison. Several professors began to teach Copernicus' theories, however, and, eventually, his new idea took hold.

THE DISCOVERIES OF TYCHO BRAHE

■ ■

Tycho Brahe (Tee-koh Bra-heh) (1546–1601) was a Dane whose first love in life was astronomy. He was raised by an uncle who wanted him to be a lawyer. He abandoned those studies in favor of astronomy as soon as his uncle died. Though he believed in astrology, Brahe began to keep accurate, scientific records of star movements.

On November 11, 1574, Brahe discovered a brilliant new star in the constellation Cassiopeia. His discovery refuted

Aristotle's belief that the stars were changeless. Although another astronomer, Wolfgang Schuler of Wittenberg, Germany, saw the new star first, the star is known as Tycho's Star. It was the discovery of a supernova, which is a star exploding and burning out at the end of its life. Although Tycho did not really understand what he was seeing, he made precise measurements of the star anyway. It did not change position but gradually faded and disappeared. He published a book, *De stella nova* (On the new star), in 1573. Brahe devoted the rest of his life to astronomy.

In 1576, King Frederick II built Tycho an observatory on Hven (now called Ven), an island in the Baltic Sea between Copenhagen and the Swedish town of Malmo. The observatory was named Uranisborg, the "Castle of the Heavens." In 1584, Tycho built another observatory that was named Stjerneborg, meaning the "Castle of the Stars." Famous scientists from all over the world came to visit and study there.

Tycho measured the positions of 777 stars and made a catalog, most of which was very accurate. He found Copernicus' theory of the sun-centered solar system hard to believe, because the stars then would have to be extremely far away. He came up with his own theory—that the sun and moon revolved around the earth, while the other planets revolved around the sun.

When Frederick II died in 1588, Tycho's funds were cut off and he lost his observatory on Hven. Taking the main instruments, he moved to Prague, in Bohemia (now Czechoslovakia), where he became Imperial Mathematician in the court of Rudolph II. Later, Hven was given to Sweden. Nothing remains of either original observatory, although a modern one is there now.

In the late 1500s, Tycho took on a partner—whose name was Johannes Kepler.

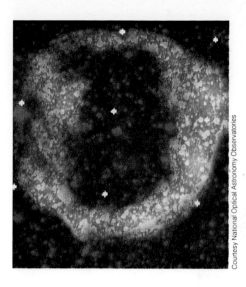

Courtesy National Optical Astronomy Observatories

This picture shows a supernova, which is a star that has exploded at the end of its life and is burning out.

Courtesy Nasa

■ ■ ■ ■ ■ ■ ■ ■ ■ ■ ■ ■

Named after the Roman messenger to the gods, Mercury is the closest planet to the sun. Mercury takes 88 earth-days to make one complete orbit around the sun. The planet is too small to have a protective atmosphere, so it is scorched by the sun during the day and is frozen at night.

THE DISCOVERY OF THE LAWS OF PLANETARY MOTION

■ ■

The movements of the planets remained foremost in most astronomers' minds. Johannes Kepler (1571–1630) was no exception.

Kepler originally planned to be a Lutheran pastor. While attending the University of Tübingen in Germany, he also studied math and became sure of Copernicus' theory that the sun was in the center of the solar system. He was asked to teach math and astronomy at Graz, in Styria, and he pursued his interest in these subjects. In 1596, he published a book, *Cosmographic Mystery*. Though most of the information was useless, he sent a copy to Tycho Brahe, who was impressed.

In 1598, all Lutheran teachers were told to leave Graz, so Kepler joined Tycho Brahe in Prague, where he became Imperial Mathematician when Tycho died. Tycho's observations and measurements of Mars gave Kepler a vital clue about the planets' orbits. He figured out that they were not circular, but *elliptical*, shaped more like a flattened circle.

Once he accepted this new idea, Kepler wrote his three Laws of Planetary Motion. The first two were published in 1609 and the third in 1618. Law 1 says that the planets orbit the sun in an elliptical pattern. Law 2 says that a planet moves fastest when it is closest to the sun. These first two laws were published in a book called *Astronomica nova* (New astronomy). Law 3 says that there is a definite connection between the size of a planet's orbit and the period it takes to go once around the sun. This law was published in *Harmonices mundi* (Harmonies of the world).

Later in life, Kepler wrote *Epitome astronomiae Copernicae* (Epitome of Copernican astronomy), which summarized his views that the sun was the center of the solar system, that the planets revolved around the sun, and that the stars were much farther away from the earth and other planets. He believed that even though the stars were at different distances, they took up a finite part of space. Nothing was beyond them, except, perhaps, a crystal sphere.

Kepler also invented a new eyepiece for a telescope. He observed a supernova in 1604, wrote a book about comets, and also wrote a science fiction novel, *Somnium* (Dream), published after he died in 1630.

Top: Kepler's first law of planetary motion says that the planets orbit the sun in an elliptical pattern. Bottom: Kepler's second law says that a planet moves fastest when it is closest to the sun. For example, because it is moving faster between points A and B, it takes the same amount of time to travel between those two points as it does between points C and D.

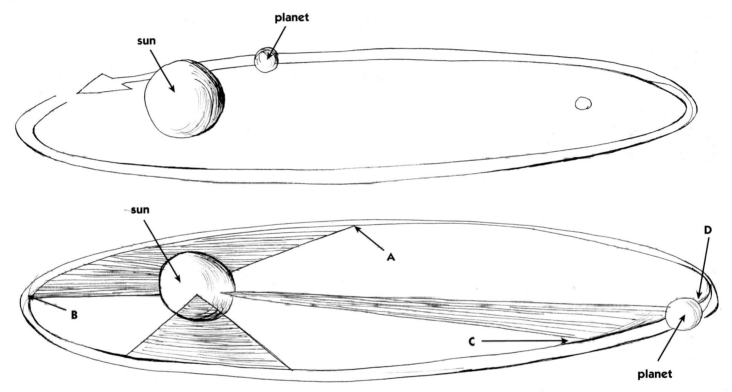

THE INVENTION OF TELESCOPIC ASTRONOMY

Galileo Galilei (1564–1642) was one of the greatest scientific pioneers.

In 1609, Galileo heard about the invention of a marvelous new instrument called the telescope. We are not sure who first invented the telescope, but history usually credits

Jan Lippersky, a Dutch lensgrinder. At the same time, an Englishman named Thomas Harriot used a telescope to look at the moon and draw a map of what he saw. However, Galileo rushed to make a telescope of his own, and because he made

Galileo Galilei was one of the world's greatest scientists. Not only did he believe that the sun was the center of our solar system at a time when this was a very unpopular view, he also discovered that there are mountains on the moon.

some fantastic discoveries with his invention, he got much of the credit for creating the telescope.

Galileo's discoveries from 1610 to 1619 mark the beginning of telescopic astronomy. He discovered that the moon has mountains and plains, which he called "seas." He described the valleys and craters and made some drawings of the moon's surface. By measuring the length of their shadows, he could tell how high the mountains were. (His numbers were a little too high, but his attempt to scientifically determine the height of the moon's mountains was an important breakthrough.)

Galileo also noticed that no matter how bright, the stars always appeared as points of light, not disks. Even our modern telescopes show them only as dots. He saw, too, that our galaxy, the Milky Way, was made up of millions and millions of stars.

Galileo was very interested in the planets. He wanted to prove that Copernicus' theory about the sun being the center of the solar system was correct. To do this, he studied the movements of the planet Venus. He saw that during the year, Venus phased from invisible to completely visible. This could only happen if Venus orbited the sun.

Then, in January of 1610, Galileo made an even more amazing discovery. He discovered that Jupiter had four moons. How could earth be the center of the universe if moons orbited Jupiter? A German named Marius also saw these four moons and named them Io, Callista, Ganymede, and Europa, names we still use today. For 370 years we did not know anything more about these moons. Then the *Voyager* missions of the late 1970s and early 1980s showed us what these moons really looked like.

After studying Jupiter, Galileo turned his attention to Saturn. In 1610, he noticed that something was odd about Saturn's shape. He thought Saturn might be two planets.

Courtesy Celestron International

■ ■ ■ ■ ■ ■ ■ ■ ■ ■ ■ ■ ■ ■ ■

This is a view of the moon as seen through a modern telescope. With the naked eye, it is possible to distinguish the moon's dark, waterless seas.

Through a telescope, Saturn appears to have solid rings. When the first spacecrafts got close enough to take pictures of the rings, the astronauts discovered that they are really made up of dust and rocks.

Two years later, all he could see was one planet. He did not understand that what he had actually seen, of course, were Saturn's rings. They disappeared in 1612 because they were edgewise to us and therefore not visible.

Galileo published his findings, which once again caused problems with the Catholic Church and with other scientists. In 1615, when he was in Florence working as the Grand Duke of Tuscany's mathematician, the Church warned Galileo that these views were heresy and that he had better alter them.

In 1629, he published a book called *Dialogue Concerning the Two Chief World Systems*. The censors approved it for publication and it appeared in February of 1632. The Pope, even though he was Galileo's old friend, was upset and called the scientist to Rome. Galileo was put on trial for heresy and found guilty. The Pope wished to force him to say that his writings were totally incorrect. Fearing death, Galileo gave in to the Church.

Galileo's research halted, and he spent the rest of his life in his villa at Arcetri.

THE DISCOVERY OF GRAVITY

What keeps the planets in their orbits and people from floating off the surface of the earth? The person who answered this question was Sir Isaac Newton (1642–1727).

A mathematician educated at Cambridge, Newton was sitting in his garden in Woolsthorpe, Lincolnshire, England, when he saw an apple fall from a tree. He wondered what pulled the apple to the ground. He realized that the force that pulled on the apple had to be the same as that which kept the moon orbiting the earth, or the earth orbiting the sun. He called this force "universal gravitation." According to this theory, every particle of matter attracts every other particle with a strength that gets weaker as the distance between them increases.

Newton realized that the moon does not fall out of orbit because it is moving. To understand this principle, imagine that you are holding a string attached to a ball. Swing the string around you and the ball will fly out and the string will pull straight and tight. If you let go of the string, the ball will fly off in one direction. Newton theorized that in just the same way, the earth pulls on the moon to keep it in orbit, and the moon does not fall toward the earth from this pull because the sun is also pulling on the moon. The force of the earth and the sun on the moon keeps it in orbit. This important theory is called Newton's "Law of Inertia."

In 1672, Newton was elected to be a Fellow of the Royal Society. Another Fellow of the Royal Society, Robert Hooke, reached the same conclusions as Newton regarding gravity. He wanted to know the precise mathematics involved, however. When he talked to Newton, he discovered that Newton had solved the problem years before but had said nothing. Not only that, Newton had lost his notes.

■ ■ ■ ■ ■ ■ ■ ■ ■ ■ ■ ■ ■ ■

After Sir Isaac Newton saw an apple fall from a tree in his garden, he formulated the theory of gravity.

Another man, Edmond Halley, who is famous for discovering the comet named after him, had Newton redo his calculations and publish them. Halley paid for the publication of Newton's book, which came out in 1687 and was called the *Principia*. This book, which took fifteen months to write, is one of the greatest books of all time. It not only discusses gravitation and the movements of the planets, the *Principia* has information about tides, as well, and it has done more for the study of astronomy than any other book since.

THE DISCOVERY OF HALLEY'S COMET

Prior to Edmond Halley (1656–1742), no one understood comets. Aristotle thought they originated on the earth and were pulled into the sky. Galileo thought comets were sunlight refracted (bent) in the earth's atmosphere. Newton thought comets traveled in straight lines rather than in elliptical orbits around the sun.

Born to a wealthy family, Halley left Oxford University before he graduated to go to the island of St. Helena, where he catalogued 381 stars. When he returned to England, Oxford granted him an honorary degree.

In 1682, Halley observed a bright comet and became very interested in the subject of comets. He collected all the recorded observations of comets seen between 1337 and 1698 and began analyzing them. He realized that comets seen in 1531 and 1607 had orbits very similar to that of the comet he saw in 1682. He wondered if this was the same comet, reappearing every seventy-six years.

Halley died in 1742, so he never got the chance to find out. On Christmas night, 1758, however, Johann Palitsch, a German amateur astronomer, spotted Halley's comet,

Courtesy National Optical Astronomy Observatories

Edmond Halley observed this bright comet in 1682. This comet returns every seventy-six years and was last seen in 1986. Called Halley's Comet after its discoverer, it won't appear again until the year 2062.

which became visible to the naked eye in 1759. Halley's comet reappeared on schedule in 1835, in 1910, and again in 1986. Records of this comet date back to 467 B.C.

In addition, Halley spent nineteen years studying the moon's movements, and he also discovered that three bright stars, Sirius, Procyon, and Arcturus, had shifted since Hipparchus had made his star catalog. In addition, Sirius had shifted since Tycho Brahe's observations at Hven. Halley knew that meant Sirius must be closer to us than the other stars were. This was the first indication of what is called "proper motion" of stars, showing that the old ideas of "fixed stars" and changeless skies were false.

THE COMET HUNTER

Edmond Halley was not the only astronomer to observe comets. The most famous comet-watcher is Charles Messier (1730–1817).

Although Messier, who was French, did not have a formal education in astronomy, he loved the field and worked for the Astronomer of the Navy. In 1759, he was assigned to watch for Halley's comet. He found the comet, but he was not allowed to announce the fact. Messier, however, became very interested in comet-hunting.

Since he was not a mathematician, Messier had his mathematical research done by a French aristocrat, Bochart de Saron. De Saron was executed in 1794, during the French Revolution, but with de Saron's calculations, Messier was able to rediscover a comet he had found the year before.

Because they looked like comets, but did not reappear and disappear, Messier was confused by star clusters and nebulae. Nebulae are very large masses of cloudlike gasses that give off light. In 1781, he catalogued these as "things to avoid" and this list is still used today.

Courtesy National Optical Astronomy Observatories

This computer-enhanced picture of Halley's Comet was taken from Chile on February 20, 1986.

3

BREAKTHROUGHS DURING THE INDUSTRIAL AGE

THE INVENTION OF LARGE TELESCOPES

The person credited as the link between the old and the new phases of astronomy is the Earl of Rosse (1800–1867), who lived at Birr Castle in Ireland. When his political career ended in 1834, he decided to build an observatory.

Up until the mid-1800s, telescopes were small devices that were not very powerful at all. These would not do for Lord Rosse. He wanted a large telescope with which he could see sights never before seen. That meant he would have to build his own, so he taught himself the art of mirror-making, and in 1838, his 36-inch (91-centimeter) telescope was completed and ready for use. It was the largest telescope in the world, but he was still not satisfied, and he started to build a 72-inch (183-centimeter) one.

In 1842, the Earl of Rosse built the largest telescope in the world. He saw farther into space than anyone had previously.

This picture shows the McMath Solar Telescope in Kitt Peak, Arizona. Many important discoveries have been made with this modern telescope.

Because making a glass mirror that large was impossible, Rosse made it out of copper and tin. He built his own furnace to melt the metal and taught employees on his estate to help him. The mirror was finished in 1842 but unfortunately broke when moved to the telescope. A second one was made and mounted between two massive stone walls. Since the telescope could not be rotated, it could follow a star for only an hour or so as it passed directly overhead.

Rosse made some important discoveries with his telescope, which operated for sixty years. Not only did he study the moon and the planets, but also some of the nebulae that Messier had catalogued. Number 51 on Messier's list was classed as a nebula, but when Rosse looked at it through the telescope, he saw that it had a spiral shape. Rosse discovered other spirals, too. He could not measure them, but he knew they were far away, that they were rotating, and that they were probably beyond our galaxy. Rosse also studied Messier's Number 1, which Rosse named the "Crab." Today, we call it the Crab Nebula.

Lord Rosse is an important figure in astronomy because he built the largest telescope the world had ever seen and he had seen farther into space than anyone had before him.

THE BUILDING OF THE LICK AND HALE OBSERVATORIES

Although Lord Rosse's telescope remained the largest telescope in the world, it eventually became old-fashioned and could not be used for the more sophisticated kinds of observations and studies of the moon and planets that were taking place in the late 1800s.

James Lick (1796–1876), who manufactured musical instruments, was very interested in astronomy. In 1874, he donated $700,000 to the University of California to build the world's most powerful telescope and the observatory that would house it. This new telescope was 36 inches (about 91 centimeters) across and was finished in 1888. Only one other telescope like it existed in the world—that one was 30 inches (76 centimeters) and was built in France in 1880. Even today, the Lick telescope is the second largest of its type in the world. The largest is the 40-inch (102-centimeter) telescope at the Yerkes Observatory, built in the year 1897 at a cost of $34,900 and paid for by Chicago businessman Charles T. Yerkes. The Yerkes Observatory is located at Williams Bay, Wisconsin.

These large telescopes and others that followed allowed astronomers to see craters and mountains on the moon, canals on Mars, and rings around Saturn. Scientists were now able to map the lunar surface. They noted that the moon had no atmosphere and therefore could have no life and no water. Not until the *Apollo* mission of 1969 did we really learn more.

Another great telescope is housed at the Hale Observatory, which is named for its founder, George Ellery Hale (1868–1938). Hale's businessman father financed his interest in astronomy and built him the Kenwood Observatory near Chicago when Hale was in college. Despite the ob-

This 120-inch (300-centimeter) Shane Reflective Telescope at the Lick Observatory became operational in 1959. Scientists salvaged what was originally the test mirror for the 200-inch (500-centimeter) telescope at Mount Palomar, polished it, and used it in the Shane Telescope.

© Gary Milburn/Tom Stack & Associates

The Hale Observatory at Mount Palomar in San Diego County, California, is one of the largest in the world.

servatory's small size, he was able to perform research there. But Hale eventually wanted a much larger telescope than his father could afford to build for him.

In 1892, Hale met Charles Yerkes. Impressed with the telescope that Yerkes was financing, Hale became the director of the observatory. As such, he was instrumental in having a 60-inch (153-centimeter) telescope built in 1908 and a 100-inch (254-centimeter) one built in November of 1917, both of which are located on Mount Wilson in California. The latter telescope, which is called the Hooker telescope after John D. Hooker of Los Angeles, who paid its $45,000 cost, was responsible for opening up whole new fields of research in astronomy. Edwin Hubble, for whom the Hubble Space Telescope is named (see chapter 4), used the telescope to determine that spiral nebulae were really distant galaxies beyond our own.

Still, Hale was not satisfied. He approached the Rockefeller Foundation for funds to build a 200-inch (500-centimeter) telescope at Mount Palomar, California. They approved six million dollars to build it. Work started in 1934, was halted by World War II, and began again in 1945. The reflector was made of a new type of glass called Pyrex, weighed 500 tons (450 metric tons), and had to be moved from Pasadena to Palomar, about 150 miles (240 km) to the south. The Hale Observatory opened on June 3, 1948, and is still in use today; it contains the second largest telescope in the world.

The Russians have a telescope 236 inches (600 centimeters) wide, which is the largest telescope in the world. Located on Mount Semirodriki near Zelenchukskaya in the Caucasus Mountains, it is powerful enough to see a lighted candle from 15,000 miles (24,000 km). Though it is driven by computer, it has not yet produced many observations of value.

THE DISCOVERY OF THE DOPPLER EFFECT

Have you ever stood alongside a railroad or subway and had a train pass you? Did you notice how the sound of the train seems high-pitched as it comes toward you, then gets lower-pitched as it goes away from you? That's because the sound waves are closer together as they come toward you and farther apart as they move away from you.

Austrian physicist and mathematician Christian Johann Doppler (1803–1853) described this effect in relation to stars in a law of physics known as the Doppler principle. To understand the principle, you must think of the spectrum of visible light. The spectrum is made up of the same array of colors as seen in a rainbow: violet, blue, green, yellow, orange, and red, in that order. Just as the sound waves of an approaching train are close together but farther apart as the train moves away, Doppler discovered that the lines in the spectrum of a star's light shift toward the violet if the star is moving toward the earth but shift toward the red if the star is moving away from the earth. By measuring this "shift," scientists can find out how fast the star is moving. These measurements are called "radial velocities."

The sound of a train seems higher pitched when the train is moving toward you than it does when the train is moving away. This is because the sound waves are closer together as they come toward you and farther apart as they move away.

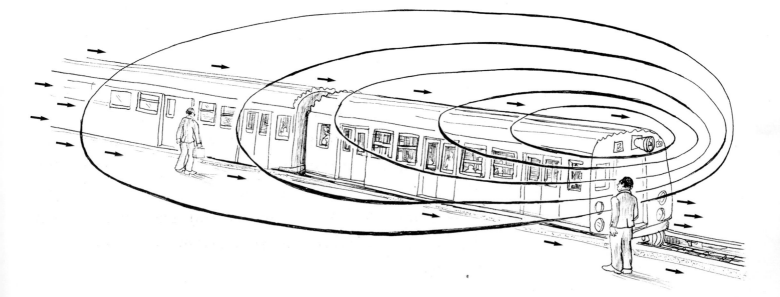

Andromeda is a spiral galaxy located over two million light-years away. Although this picture was taken through a telescope, the Andromeda Galaxy is the most distant object in the sky that can be seen with the naked eye.

THE DISCOVERY OF OTHER GALAXIES

As telescopes got more and more powerful, a scientist named William Herschel (1738–1822) was able to see that perhaps some of the objects in space that Rosse had characterized as "nebulae" might actually be separate systems far beyond our own galaxy, which is called the Milky Way. His idea was not popular, however, and it was not pursued again until 1920.

At that time, two American astronomers, Harlow Shapley (1885–1972) and Heber D. Curtis (1872–1942), had a debate. Shapley felt that the spirals were part of our own galaxy, which he had measured as a certain size. Curtis felt that the galaxy was smaller than that and that the spirals were separate systems. They were both partially right. The galaxy is as big as Shapley claimed, and the spirals are separate galaxies, as Curtis believed.

Edwin Hubble (1889–1953), an astronomer who worked at both the Yerkes and Mount Wilson observatories, decided to look for "Cepheid" stars in the spirals. Cepheid stars, also called variable stars, are unstable and shrink and swell. Astronomers can determine the distance of these stars very easily, because their brightness is not constant. They get fainter, then brighter, then fainter, then brighter, and so on. Some go through their cycles in a matter of days, while others require years. For instance, Eta Aquilae goes from its brightest to its faintest over a period of seven days.

Hubble found Cepheids in the Andromeda spiral. The stars were much too far away to be part of our galaxy. He estimated the distance at 750,000 light-years, though that number was raised to 900,000 later on, then to 2,200,000 light-years.

THE DISCOVERY OF RADIOASTRONOMY

■■■■■■■■■■■■■■■■■■■■■■■■■■■■■■■■■■■

Although Hubble's measurements of light from Cepheid stars were extremely valuable, visible light makes up only a small portion of the total range of wavelengths, or electromagnetic spectrum. In this spectrum, we have many kinds of light rays: ultraviolet rays, X rays, gamma rays, and infrared rays. Beyond light rays, there are radio waves.

While light rays easily reach the earth, most radio waves are blocked by the earth's atmosphere. Now that we have satellites, picking up these radio waves is no problem. An important discovery was made, however, back in 1931, when no space-based equipment was available.

An American, Karl Guthe Jansky (1905–1949), who worked for the Bell Telephone Laboratories, did research about problems with shortwave radio communication, especially static. He set up a radio aerial on a New Jersey farm and heard radio noise from a nearby storm and from storms farther away. Then he heard a different kind of noise—a very weak, steady hiss. This noise seemed to come from a definite place in the sky, which seemed to be different from day to day. Jansky finally found the answer—the source of the sound was the Milky Way itself.

■ ■ ■ ■ ■ ■ ■ ■ ■ ■ ■ ■ ■ ■

With his original radio aerial, called "the Merry-go-round," Karl Jansky discovered sounds coming from the Milky Way.

Jansky believed that the noise came from the very heart of the galaxy, in Sagittarius, and published his results on May 5, 1933. Like many scientists before him, Jansky had come up with a new invention—in his case, the field of radioastronomy—but he never did anything with his discovery other than publish a few more results in 1937.

Others were left to carry on this work, most notably Sir Bernard Lovell, who designed a radiotelescope with a "dish" antenna 250 feet (76 m) in diameter, which is set up at the Jodrell Bank Research Laboratories near Manchester, England. Even though it is not the largest radiotelescope in the world, Jodrell Bank has done as much for radioastronomy as Mount Wilson and Mount Palomar have for visual astronomy.

This picture of the Milky Way Galaxy was obtained from a NASA satellite. Viewed from the side, as this picture shows, our galaxy appears to be a saucer-shaped disk. (Viewed from the top, it looks like a spiral.) The bulge in the middle shows how the center of the galaxy is crowded with stars.

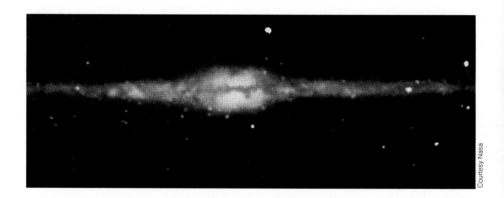

Courtesy Nasa

THEORIES ON THE ORIGIN OF THE UNIVERSE

In the 1600s, an Irish archbishop, James Ussher (1581–1656), attempted to resolve the contradictions between the Christian belief that God created the universe, called the creationist view, and the facts emerging from the new science of astronomy by declaring that the earth was created by a divine power at 9 A.M. on October 23, 4004 B.C. He arrived at this very specific date by adding up all the ages of the great people mentioned in the Bible.

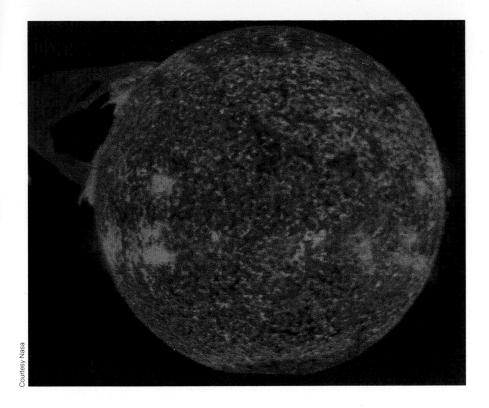

Courtesy Nasa

The sun is thought to be five billion years old. This photograph of the sun, taken December 19, 1973, shows one of the most spectacular solar flares (in the upper left corner) ever recorded. A solar flare is a sudden and distinct brightening of the surface of the sun. Solar flares occur quite often; small ones last for a few minutes, while large ones last for several hours.

Today, we know that the sun is about five billion years old—and about halfway through its life. We know that the earth is about 4½ billion years old. Scientists have three main theories on how the universe was created: the Big Bang theory, the Oscillating Universe theory, and the Steady State theory.

■ The Big Bang Theory

The Big Bang theory was developed by Belgian abbot Georges Lemaitre (1894–1966) in the 1920s. He felt that all the matter in the universe started at the same time, about 15 billion years ago, from one atom that exploded outward in all directions for billions of years until the universe measured about one billion light-years across. When it reached that point, it stopped expanding.

Lemaitre also felt that there was an opposite force to gravitation called *cosmic repulsion*. He believed the repulsion and gravitation pushed and pulled on all the matter in the universe until the galaxies and planets were formed.

Over the years, this theory has been modified and refined by other scientists, such as astrophysics pioneer Sir Arthur Eddington of England and George Gamow of the United States.

There are some problems with this theory. If the universe started at a certain point, what happened before that? And if the universe had a beginning, and is now going through a middle, will it have an end someday, too?

■ The Oscillating Universe Theory

The Oscillating Universe theory is a variation of the Big Bang theory. This theory states that after the initial Big Bang, all the matter in the universe rushed out for 60 to 80 million years, then slowed down, stopped, and rushed back to where it came from for another 60 to 80 million years. According to the theory, at this time another Big Bang occurred and the process started all over again. So over the course of the history of the universe, there have been many Big Bangs, and not just one.

■ ■ ■ ■ ■ ■ ■ ■ ■ ■ ■ ■ ■ ■

Belgian abbott George Lemaitre believed all matter in the universe originated billions of years ago with a ''big bang,'' when one atom exploded in all directions. According to the Big Bang theory, this matter is still expanding. Scientists think that someday the universe will stop expanding and will begin to collapse in on itself.

■ The Steady State Theory

The third theory is the Steady State theory, which was developed by Hermann Bondi and Thomas Gold in 1948 at Cambridge University in England. They did not think that any type of creation was involved—not even a big bang-type creation. They believed that the universe has always existed and will always exist in the form it is now. Old galaxies are always disappearing, and new galaxies are always appearing out of nothingness.

Two major problems exist with this theory. Since galaxies take millions or billions of years to form, the theory cannot be tested, nor can it explain how the universe originally came into being; it claims that the universe just appeared. The theory fell into disfavor from research showing that the universe is indeed always changing and therefore cannot be in a steady state.

In 1965, Arno Penzias and Robert Wilson, who worked for the Bell Telephone Laboratories, discovered microwave radiation with an intensity measuring three degrees above absolute zero coming from all parts of the sky. Astronomers believe that this is what is left of the Big Bang itself. Penzias and Wilson received the Nobel prize for their important discovery.

Does their discovery mean that the Big Bang is right? Not necessarily. Our knowledge of the universe is limited because our technology is limited. Only in this century have we developed technology to let us leave our planet. Perhaps we have as many mistaken ideas as the people in Aristotle's time, who thought that the earth must be the center of the universe that ended with the stars just a few miles overhead. Maybe the Hubble Space Telescope (see chapter 4) will offer some more clues, or perhaps answers will not come until we have the ability to travel across the galaxy at superlight speed.

Courtesy Nasa

The information gathered from the Hubble Space Telescope may provide us with more clues on the origin of the universe. This picture shows the Hubble Space Telescope on the arm of the space shuttle.

4

BREAKTHROUGHS DURING THE SPACE AGE

THE DISCOVERY OF BLACK HOLES

■ ■

Ever since the Marquis de Laplace (1749–1827) first suggested the idea of black holes in 1798, we have been fascinated by this strange phenomenon in space. What are they really besides a void in space where there are no stars? Can they really be doors to other universes or time tunnels, as one astronomer holds to be true? Is it true that time travels backward in a black hole?

We believe now that black holes are massive stars collapsing under their own gravitational force. Their matter is escaping at the speed of light. Since the star is collapsing, the light cannot escape but falls in on itself. Unfortunately, because we cannot see these stars, we know very little about what is happening to them. They just show up as empty "black holes" in space.

■ ■ ■ ■ ■ ■ ■ ■ ■ ■ ■ ■ ■ ■

A black hole is a massive star that is collapsing in on itself. Matter that comes near it is dragged into the black hole and can never escape.

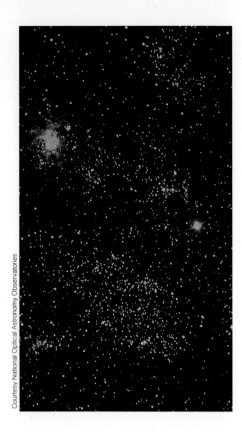

Courtesy National Optical Astronomy Observatories

■ ■ ■ ■ ■ ■ ■ ■ ■ ■ ■ ■ ■ ■

This photograph shows a supernova, which is the explosion of a very large star. When this happens, the star can become millions or billions of times brighter. Scientists think that a neutron star, an incredibly dense celestial object, is left after a star goes supernova.

Some scientists believe that at the perimeter of the black hole, time itself stands still, and inside the hole, the directions of space and time are interchanged. In the hole's center, there is antigravity, and around the hole, you have to travel at the speed of light to remain in the same place.

The simplest black holes have only two parts: a "singularity" surrounded by an "event horizon." The black hole is completely empty. All of the star's matter has been crushed into the singularity, the center of the mass. The outer edge of the black hole is the event horizon, where all time stops. When anything crosses the event horizon, it has no chance to turn back but is pulled toward the singularity. Inside the event horizon, the directions of space and time are reversed.

The equations describing these simple black holes were developed by German astronomer Karl Schwartzchild in 1916, so simple black holes are called Schwartzchild black holes. These have no electric charge and do not rotate.

Between 1916 and 1918, H. Reissner in Germany and G. Nordstrom in Denmark theorized that there might be electrically charged black holes. These are now called Reissner-Nordstrom black holes. They claimed that if a static black hole received an electric charge, that as the charge grew, a second outer event horizon would be created. As the charge increases, the inner event horizon grows stronger, while the outer one shrinks. When the event horizons merge, the maximum charge occurs.

Black holes can also rotate. As they do, they drag space and time around themselves. From a safe distance, the amount of spin can be measured.

Are these theories correct? No doubt there are many things in the universe that will surprise us as time goes by. We cannot really know what is inside a black hole because we cannot yet go there to find out.

THE DISCOVERY OF QUASARS AND PULSARS

The word "quasar" is an acronym (letters that stand for a set of words) for "*quas*istell*ar*" radio sources. Scientists discovered quasars in the late 1950s using radio telescopes that detected radio waves originating from points in space. Quasars send out a tremendous amount of energy as light and radio waves.

The Mount Palomar telescope played an important role in this discovery. In 1960, American astronomer Rudolph Minkow used this telescope and found that these signals came from blue, starlike objects. The lines of the spectrum of a quasar are shifted more toward the red than any other known object, which means that quasars are farther away than any other objects in the sky.

Quasars resemble stars, but are much farther away. They emit incredibly large amounts of light and radio waves and are a trillion times brighter than our sun.

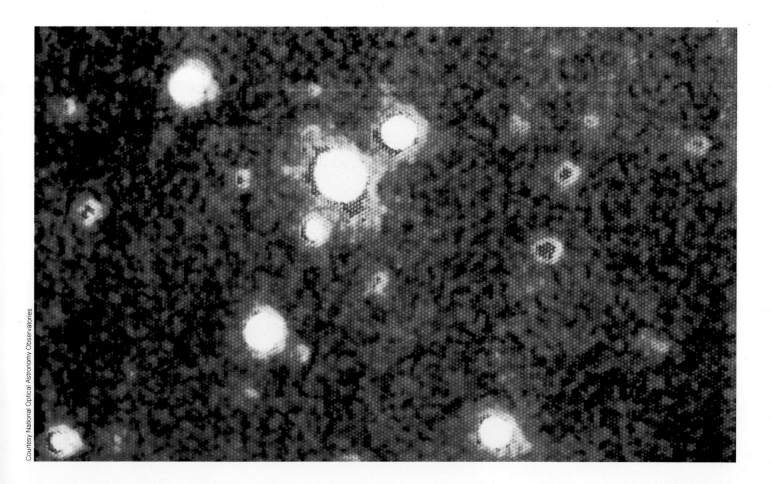

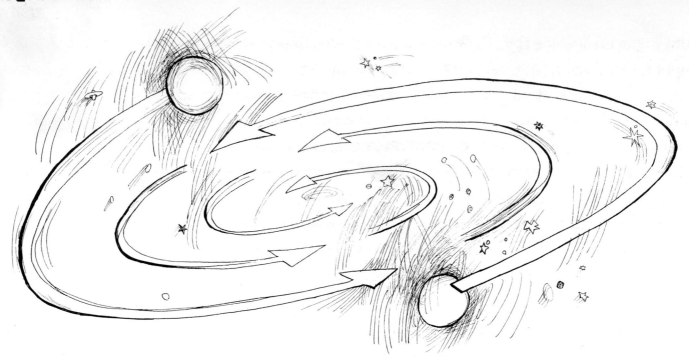

■ ■ ■ ■ ■ ■ ■ ■ ■ ■ ■ ■ ■ ■

Scientists have recently found a binary pulsar. Two dense stars, one a pulsar, the other an unknown object, are circling one another. Gravity is pulling these two stars closer and closer together, and eventually they will merge. Their combined mass will then be too great, and the two stars will disappear into a black hole.

Scientists believe the farthest known quasar is about 10 billion light-years away. Even though quasars are less than one light-year in size, they generate more radio energy and light than one hundred galaxies like the Milky Way and are a trillion times brighter than the sun.

British astronomers Fred Hoyle (1915–) and Geoffrey Ronald Burbridge (1925–) think that quasars are pieces of explosions of other galaxies near the Milky Way, but they have no proof of this.

Pulsars are also sources of radio energy, but in the form of pulses. Scientists think that pulsars are rotating neutron stars with diameters of about 10 miles (26 km). A neutron star is what is left after a star goes supernova. Neutron stars consist mostly of closely packed neutrons and are the densest kind of matter so far discovered. To compare, if something as small as the ball of a ballpoint pen were packed with neutrons, it would contain more than 100,000 tons (90,000 metric tons) of mass.

In November of 1967, Jocelyn Bell at Cambridge University in England detected a strange radio source. She could not see it but could tell it was ticking very quickly. Along with the team she worked with, she thought these signals might be artificial ones from another world many light-years away. Finally, the team discovered that the ticking came from a neutron star. This was the first pulsar. The team soon found another in the Crab Nebula.

In 1969, at the Steward Observatory in Arizona, a team of scientists saw the pulsar in the Crab Nebula. It was a very faint, flashing object. Several other pulsars were found. Their ticks were also caused by the rotation of a neutron star. These stars have powerful magnetic fields, and as electrons on their surface meet those fields at their north and south poles, the electrons are beamed outwards like a rotating searchlight, emitting radio waves we can detect. We receive a pulse every time the "beam" of the spinning neutron star sweeps across us.

THE FIRST MAN ON THE MOON

"That's one small step for a man; one giant leap for mankind." With those words, American astronaut Neil Armstrong became the first human to set foot on the moon.

For thousands of years, people had wondered what the moon was made of. We knew it had craters and mountains and valleys. Was it solid or soft? And what did the dark side look like? Only in this century did it become possible for us to find out.

In 1961, when President John F. Kennedy committed the United States to "sending a man to the moon and returning him safely to the earth" by 1969, even some of the aerospace engineers who were to work on this ambitious project thought that it was impossible.

Before men landed on the moon, however, the Russians had sent several space probes there. Thomas Gold, who at the time was an astronomer at the Royal Greenwich Ob-

On July 16, 1969, *Apollo 11* rose above its mobile launcher at the Kennedy Space Center. This signalled the beginning of human-kind's first trip to land on the moon.

Courtesy Nasa

Courtesy Nasa

■ ■ ■ ■ ■ ■ ■ ■ ■ ■ ■ ■ ■ ■

In this photograph, *Apollo 11*'s lunar landing module (LM), with Neil Armstrong and Buzz Aldrin aboard, heads for the surface of the moon. This picture was taken from the command module. The earth is visible in the background.

servatory in England, thought that sending probes was a waste of time. He believed that the surface of the moon was soft dust and that the probes would just sink through and disappear.

In February of 1966, the Russians sent up *Luna 9*. Its drop to the moon was slowed by rocket braking, and as we know, it landed on a hard surface. This reassured everyone, especially the astronauts who were to fly to the moon. From 1966 to 1968, seven American *Surveyor* probes and five *Orbiter* probes were also sent to the moon. The *Orbiter* probes took pictures of the dark side of the moon, which, unlike the light side, turned out to have no dark, waterless seas at all.

We still did not know anything about what the craters really were, however. In July 1969, *Apollo 11* carried Neil Armstrong, Buzz Aldrin, and Michael Collins on their historic trip to the moon. Armstrong and Aldrin had three hours of oxygen in their tanks, and during that short time, they collected soil samples, then headed back to their vessel. Hard work and diligence had paid off. Kennedy's goal had been reached.

Though the moon itself is lifeless, as astronomers had suspected, vegetables grown in moon dust in experiments performed here on earth have grown several times larger than they do in earth soil.

Six more Apollo missions followed *Apollo 11* to the moon. From these missions we learned that the moon, which is the same age as the earth, 4½ billion years old, is not cold and rigid all the way through as previously believed. Like the earth, the moon has a crust, mantle, and core. The outermost part of the moon is called *regolith*. This loose layer is 3 to 66 feet (1–20 m) deep. Below that is

Courtesy Nasa

■ ■ ■ ■ ■ ■ ■ ■ ■ ■ ■ ■ ■

Neil Armstrong and Buzz Aldrin first walked on the moon on July 20, 1969. In this picture, Buzz Aldrin sets up an experiment to measure earthquake activity on the moon.

a layer of broken-up rock about 0.6 mile (1 km) deep, and below that is about 15 miles (25 km) of solid rock. The crust is 27 to 40 miles (45–65 km) deep. Below the crust is the mantle, which is about 600 miles (1,000 km) deep, then a region that is partially melted and called the *asthenosphere*, and finally the core, which is heavy and molten, and probably very rich in iron. The seas, or *maria*, are lava plains. Despite their name, they are waterless. The most common material there is the volcanic rock basalt. The highland rocks have less iron than the rocks in the seas, but have more calcium and aluminum. Seismometers left on the moon have shown that the moon has moonquakes just as the earth has earthquakes.

No one has gone back to the moon since the last Apollo flight, but plans are to eventually set up mining colonies there. Humankind is on the verge of becoming a spacefaring species.

THE HUBBLE SPACE TELESCOPE

Are there planets around other stars? How old is the universe? What exactly are black holes?

For years, scientists and science fiction writers alike have dreamed of having a giant telescope in space that will let us determine the answers to these and many other questions that are currently unanswerable.

Back in the early 1920s, rocket pioneer Herman Oberth spoke of the benefits of such a telescope and described his idea for what would later become the Hubble Space Telescope. As we have already discussed, Edwin Hubble, after whom the telescope was eventually named, proved that there are other galaxies beyond our own Milky Way (see chapter 3). After World War II, interest in a large space telescope began to grow.

The Apollo missions paved the way for the space shuttle flights. The space shuttle is the United States' current vehicle for taking astronauts into space.

Courtesy Nasa

Courtesy Nasa

On the thirty-fifth flight of the space shuttle, the *Discovery* mission on April 25, 1990, that dream became a reality. The Hubble Space Telescope was launched from *Discovery*'s cargo bay.

Why do we need a telescope in space? The main reason is that the atmosphere around the earth prevents us from seeing beyond certain distances. Putting a telescope beyond the atmosphere means the view will be unobstructed, and therefore clear. In fact, Hubble's viewing

This picture shows the Hubble Space Telescope on the arm of the space shuttle before its release.

This picture shows vapor cloud formations from a NASA rocket that was fired off an island in Virginia. Visible over much of the eastern coast of the United States, many people mistook the colored clouds for UFOs.

ability is designed to be seven to ten times greater than that of earth-based telescopes. This means Hubble can see objects up to 14 billion light-years away. A light-year is how far light travels in a year. That means that if Hubble is seeing something 14 billion light-years away, that image left its point of origin 14 billion years ago.

Orbiting far above the earth, Hubble is expected to revolutionize astronomy with discoveries that will be as important as Galileo's discovery that the earth orbited the sun or Newton's discovery of the law of gravity. Not only will it be able to help us determine the age of the universe by dating the most ancient star in the center of star clusters, but it may be able to study those light waves that originate from the Big Bang.

Built at a cost of $1.5 billion, Hubble has eight cameras. With this powerful equipment, it can take pictures of stars that are twenty-five times fainter than the dimmest object visible from the earth.

Hubble will study different types of stars, black holes, and the activity of quasars and radio galaxies. Hubble will also observe nebulae, monitor the state of the planets in our system, and look for the presence of planets around other stars.

Unfortunately, the Hubble experiments have not gone as planned. Some instruments were out of focus, and computer problems appeared. To make matters worse, scientists rapidly discovered that the mirrors on the Space Telescope were made backwards and could not work properly. These problems are being resolved, however, by sending a shuttle mission to replace the faulty parts.

Despite its problems, the Hubble Telescope has supplied scientists with information that could never have been gathered before and promises to revolutionize the study of astronomy.

We will learn a lot more secrets about the universe from Hubble. Some of them may upset many people. For instance, we may think that people in the 1600s were silly for not wanting to accept that the earth was not the center of the solar system. Some of our religions today, however, teach that humans are the only people God has created and that earth is the only planet with life. What happens if Hubble is able to discover life elsewhere in the galaxy?

Even though we have learned a lot about the universe over the last few hundred years, we must remember that we are just one little planet around a not-very-important star at the outer edge of the galaxy. A whole intergalactic community of intelligent life may exist out there that is totally unaware that we exist. *Or is it*? We have certainly had enough UFO sightings to suggest that somebody out there knows we are here. They probably also have learned that most humans are not psychologically ready to learn that we are not alone. Someday, perhaps soon, we may be ready for such a profound shock.

■ ■ ■ ■ ■ ■ ■ ■ ■ ■ ■ ■ ■ ■

People from all over the world have reported seeing UFOs. There are even scientists and trained observers who are hunting for UFOs and performing studies about them. This is a photograph of a supposed UFO taken by a man in California. Perhaps the Hubble Telescope, or some technology of the future, will show us if there really is other intelligent life existing in the universe.

BIBLIOGRAPHY

◼◼◼◼◼◼◼◼◼◼◼◼◼◼◼◼

Asimov, Isaac. *Asimov's Guide to Halley's Comet*. New York: Walker and Company, 1985.

———*The Exploding Suns: The Secrets of Supernovas*. New York: E.P. Dutton, Inc., 1985.

———*Counting the Eons*. Garden City, New York: Doubleday and Co., Inc., 1983.

Aveni, Anthony, ed. *Archeoastronomy in Precolumbian America*. Austin, Texas: University of Texas Press, 1977.

Barrow, John D., and Joseph Silk. *The Left Hand of Creation: The Origin and Evolution of the Expanding Universe*. New York: Basic Books, Inc., 1983.

Black, David C., ed. *Project Orion: A Design Study of a System for Detecting Extrasolar Planets*. Washington, D.C.: National Aeronautics and Space Administration, 1980.

Calder, Nigel. *The Comet is Coming: The Feverish Legacy of Mr. Halley*. New York: Penguin Books, 1980.

Dietz, David. *Stars and the Universe*. New York: Random House Science Library, Random House, Inc., 1968.

Disney, Michael. *The Hidden Universe*. New York: MacMillan Publishing Company, 1984.

Durham, Frank, and Robert D. Purrington. *Frame of the Universe*. New York: Columbia University Press, 1983.

Flaste, Richard, et al. *The New York Times Guide to the Return of Halley's Comet*. New York: Times Books, a Division of Random House, 1985.

Greenstein, George. *The Symbiotic Universe: Life and Mind in the Cosmos*. New York: William Morrow and Company, Inc., 1988.

Kaufman, William J. *Black Holes and Warped Spacetime*. San Francisco: W. H. Freeman and Company, 1979.

Mallove, Eugene T. *The Quickening Universe: Cosmic Evolution and Human Destiny*. New York: St. Martin's Press, 1987.

Menzel, Donald H. *Astronomy*. New York: Random House, Inc., 1978.

Mitton, Jacqueline. *Astronomy: An Introduction for the Amateur Astronomer*. New York: Charles Scribner's Sons, 1978.

Moore, Patrick. *History of Astronomy*. London: MacDonald and Company, 1983.

Morse, Joseph Laffan. *Funk & Wagnalls New Encyclopedia*. Vols. 3, 7, 8, 14, 15, 19, 20, 21, 22, 24, 25. New York: Funk & Wagnalls, Inc., 1973.

Sullivan, Walter. *Black Holes: The Edge of Space, the Edge of Time*. Garden City, New York: Anchor Press, Doubleday, 1979.

Whipple, Fred L. *Orbiting the Sun: Planets and Satellites of the Solar System*. Cambridge, Massachusetts: Harvard University Press, 1981.

INDEX

◼◼◼◼◼◼◼◼◼◼◼◼◼◼◼